R-U-N

(An Adventure)

JUNE DEMERLING

Tellwell Talent
www.tellwell.ca

ISBN
978-0-2288-4282-8 (Hardcover)
978-0-2288-4281-1 (Paperback)

This story is dedicated to three special people:

Kirk, Erika, and Lili

Story written by June Demerling

Edited by Jen

Illustrated by Stephanie

Special thanks to my children, my grandchildren and
my siblings for making every day an adventure.

This story was inspired by a childhood memory

Beth was only six years old, a bright, energetic strawberry blonde. Ann was her-five-year-old sister, a bit smaller and blonde, but just as energetic. They lived in the country and loved country life with its huge out-doors, no neighbours, but lots of nature to see and play with. They both had huge imaginations, so there was never a dull moment. There were caterpillars to play with, frogs to watch, dragonflies and many other fascinating animals and insects to discover. Adventure was their middle name.

It was a beautiful sunny day, inviting adventure. The warm, late spring sun filled the earth with happiness. This was a day that Beth and Ann had been waiting for.

The gentle breeze beckoned, "Come play with me." The buttercups nodded their heads in agreement and the butterflies flapped their wings in glee. The many coloured grasses in the fields and valley were waving at the children to come to the meadow. The meadow was a pleasant place to play, enjoy the warmth of the sunbeams, and listen to the whispers of the breeze.

Beth and Ann were looking for adventure. They believed they might just find it if they followed the gentle breeze.

The meadow was so pleasant and inviting that it was easy to forget the dangers that might lurk there. The meadow was also a place where the neighbours' cattle graze and sometimes, even the Hereford bull was there. He did not like sharing his space with outsiders. This did not deter the girls, as they were bound for adventure. Beth and Ann, hand in hand, skipped down the valley and greeted the flowers, butterflies and grasses as they went while the breezes whispered gentle encouragement in their ears. They ran up the gentle rising hill to the meadow.

The meadow is a huge inviting green space to romp, play, and sing. As they approached the old rail fence surrounding the meadow, Beth looked one way, Ann looked the other, and then they both looked the opposite direction. It never hurts to be extra careful. Today there was nothing in sight!

They clambered over the fence and started to sing and dance. It was such fun, just nature and the girls. What a wonderful adventure for Beth and Ann: talking to the flowers, whispering to the breezes, singing and dancing with the birds. The meadow was such a wonderful, big area for the children to play and they were only in the centre of the field. Time seemed to pass quickly and yet stand still.

Thud, thud, snort, thud, thud!

What was that? The girls looked at each other in terror. Out of the corner of her eye, Beth spotted something moving fast. It was coming towards them like a freight train, a blur of colour! It was the Hereford bull!

R-U-N! With hearts pounding, their breathing quickened and became heavy. The breezes called faster, faster. Their legs moved like their feet were on fire. They were in full motion. Beth hollered breathlessly to Ann, "The tree by fence!" The bull was gaining on them.

Out of breath and stamina dwindling, Beth clambered hastily up the old apple tree. Ann, being a little smaller and a little slower, slid behind the tree. The tree was such a good friend always willing to help! The bull snorted; Beth could feel its breath on her legs. It slowed, turned and commenced grazing. As he lost a little more interest, Ann had caught her breath and climbed up the tree to a branch beside Beth. Their hearts stopped pounding and their breathing slowed to normal again.

The girls, with their legs dangling comfortably from the branches, were delighted to continue their conversation. They thanked the tree for its help. Once again, they turned their interest to the sun, the breezes and the birds with the flowers nodding in approval. Beth and Ann rejoined the bird's chorus, heartily enjoying themselves, animated with delight.

Time had passed and daylight was dwindling away. It was time to return home for supper, back to reality. The girls jumped down from the apple tree, climbed back over the fence, and headed for home. They bid farewell to the birds, waved good-bye to the grasses and said good night to the buttercups.

The flowers replied, "Thank you for coming."
The breezes said, "So long until another day."

With a twinkle in their eyes and a wry grin across their faces, Beth and Ann turned and said, "Good night, Mr. Bull."

It had been a wonderful day of fun and adventure and it was coming to an end. The girls skipped and sang all the way home, happy and exhausted from their day of adventure.

CPSIA information can be obtained
at www.ICGtesting.com
Printed in the USA
LVHW051801050121
675685LV00044B/2206